# Business Intelligence

Latest Strategies to Solve Real-World Business Problems

Ghazwan Alemara

**Copyright © 2024 Ghazwan Alemara. All rights reserved.**

No part of this publication may be reproduced, distributed, or transmitted in any form or by any means, including photocopying, recording, or other electronic or mechanical methods, without the prior written permission of the publisher, except in the case of brief quotations embodied in critical reviews and certain other noncommercial uses permitted by copyright law.

For permissions requests or inquiries, please contact the publisher at hello@ghazwanalemara.com

**Published by ghazwanalemara.com**

# Contents

Contents ................................................................... 3
Introduction ............................................................... 1
The Foundations of Business Intelligence ............................... 6
    What is Business Intelligence (BI)? ............................... 6
    How Data Transforms into Actionable Insights ................. 9
    Common Tools and Technologies ................................ 13
Implementing BI Strategies Across Business Functions ........... 19
    Marketing with Data: Customer Insights and Trends ... 19
    Financial Analytics: Optimizing Cost and Revenue ...... 25
    Supply Chain and Operations Optimization ................. 29
Data-Driven Leadership and Decision Making ....................... 37
    The Role of Executives in a BI-Driven Business ........... 37
    Strategic BI Use in High-Stakes Decision-Making ........ 41
    Challenges in Shifting to Data-Driven Leadership ........ 45
Real-World Case Studies in Business Intelligence ................... 51
    Small Businesses Using BI to Grow ............................. 51
    Global Enterprises Thriving with BI ............................. 55
    Lessons Learned from BI Failures ................................ 59
Overcoming Common BI Challenges ..................................... 65
    Breaking Down Data Silos for Seamless Integration ..... 65
    Ensuring Data Quality and Accuracy ........................... 69
    Managing Data Privacy and Ethical Concerns .............. 74
Leveraging BI for Future Growth ........................................... 79
    Predictive Analytics: Anticipating the Future ................ 79

  BI in Emerging Markets ................................................... 83
  AI and Machine Learning in BI ....................................... 88
Actionable Strategies for Implementing BI ........................... 95
  Creating a BI-Driven Culture ......................................... 95
  Customizing BI Solutions for Your Business .................. 99
  Scaling BI Solutions as Your Business Grows ............. 103
Conclusion ............................................................................ 108

# Introduction

Imagine this: you're leading a fast-growing company and need to make a critical decision about entering a new market. Should you dive in based on instinct, or would you rather rely on insights derived from analyzing millions of data points, uncovering patterns that no human could detect unaided? In today's business world, the latter is not just an option—it's a necessity. Welcome to the era of Business Intelligence (BI), where data isn't just collected but transformed into a strategic asset that can revolutionize your decision-making process.

Business Intelligence is not a new concept, but its importance has skyrocketed in the digital age. Companies like Amazon and Netflix thrive on data—using it to predict customer behavior, optimize operations, and even innovate in ways competitors struggle to replicate. However, this book isn't about marveling at the tech giants. It's about providing **you** with the tools, strategies, and knowledge to leverage BI, no matter the size or stage of your business. Whether you're managing a small startup or navigating a global enterprise, the power of data-driven decisions is within your reach.

**Purpose of the Book**

This book is designed to help business leaders, managers, and decision-makers harness the full potential of Business Intelligence. Our goal is simple: to demystify BI and provide you with actionable strategies to solve real-world business challenges using the latest BI techniques. You'll gain practical insights into using data analytics to make smarter decisions, optimize processes, and drive innovation in your organization.

**Why This Topic Matters Now**

The business landscape is more competitive than ever, and those who can turn data into actionable insights will have a clear advantage. In recent years, the explosion of data—from customer interactions, operational metrics, and digital platforms—has created both opportunities and challenges. Companies that successfully use BI to sift through the noise and focus on what matters are not just surviving but thriving. This book arrives at a critical juncture when many businesses are still struggling to fully implement effective BI strategies, making this information timely and essential.

**Structure of the Book**

*Business Intelligence: Latest Strategies to Solve Real-World Business Problems* is divided into seven chapters, each designed to tackle a specific aspect of BI. From understanding foundational principles to learning about the latest tools and technologies, this book will guide you step-by-step through the process of incorporating BI into your organization.

- In Chapter 1, you'll be introduced to the fundamentals of BI and how it converts raw data into actionable insights.

- Chapter 2 delves into how BI strategies can be applied across different business functions like marketing, finance, and operations.

- In Chapter 3, we focus on how executives and managers can use BI for high-stakes decision-making.

- Chapter 4 offers real-world case studies from companies that have successfully implemented BI, highlighting both successes and challenges.

- Chapter 5 addresses common BI challenges such as data silos and data quality issues, offering solutions to overcome them.

- In Chapter 6, you'll explore advanced topics like predictive analytics, artificial intelligence, and their roles in shaping the future of BI.

- Finally, Chapter 7 gives you actionable strategies for implementing BI within your organization, no matter your current stage of data maturity.

## Setting the Tone

This book is written in a conversational, accessible style that aims to break down complex topics into digestible insights. We'll avoid technical jargon where possible, but we won't shy away from diving deep into the strategies and tools that will make a real impact on your business. Our tone is practical, forward-thinking, and results-oriented, making it perfect for busy professionals who need actionable advice now.

## Why Keep Reading?

By the end of this book, you won't just understand Business Intelligence—you'll know how to implement it. You'll have the confidence to make data-driven decisions, the tools to execute those strategies, and the insights to stay ahead in an increasingly competitive business environment. Whether you're looking to optimize your current operations, break into new markets, or simply improve decision-making within your company, this book will serve as your guide.

Let's unlock the power of data together. Welcome to the future of business intelligence.

Chapter 1

# The Foundations of Business Intelligence

## What is Business Intelligence (BI)?

At its core, BI is the process of transforming data into actionable insights that help businesses make informed decisions. Every organization collects vast amounts of data, whether it's customer transactions, website traffic, or internal operations. BI systems and tools take this raw data, clean it up, analyze it, and present it in a way that helps decision-makers understand patterns, trends, and opportunities.

To put it simply, BI acts as the bridge between data and decision-making. Without BI, data is just a collection of numbers sitting in spreadsheets or databases, often too complex for leaders to interpret and use effectively. BI tools convert that data into visual reports, dashboards, and summaries that reveal the stories behind the numbers—stories that can guide business strategies.

**The Role of Data in BI**

Business Intelligence thrives on data. Think of data as the raw material. It could come from sales figures, website visits, social media interactions, or even machine performance in a manufacturing plant. BI tools take all this data from various sources, process it, and then present the findings in a way that is easy to understand. This allows companies to spot patterns that wouldn't be obvious from a quick glance at the raw numbers.

For example, a retail company might notice, through BI analysis, that certain products sell better during specific seasons or that customers from certain regions prefer certain items. Armed with this insight, they can tailor their marketing efforts and adjust inventory to meet demand more efficiently.

**BI Tools and Technologies**

BI isn't just about crunching numbers; it relies on sophisticated tools and technologies to gather and process data. Tools like Power BI, Tableau, and Google Analytics are some of the most popular BI platforms used by businesses today. These platforms provide users with interactive dashboards, customizable reports, and data visualization tools that allow them to analyze information in real-time. They help organizations see trends at a glance, offering valuable insights into customer behavior, operational inefficiencies, and market opportunities.

These tools are particularly useful because they are designed for users with varying levels of technical expertise. Business leaders don't need to be data scientists to use BI tools—they just need to know how to read and interpret the insights the tools provide.

**Why Business Intelligence Matters**

In today's world, where competition is fierce and markets change rapidly, making data-driven decisions can be the difference between thriving and falling behind. BI gives businesses a competitive edge by enabling them to act based on facts, not assumptions. This is particularly important in industries where customer preferences change quickly, or where efficiency is critical to maintaining profit margins.

Moreover, BI helps companies become more proactive rather than reactive. Instead of waiting for problems to arise, businesses can use BI to predict challenges, identify potential areas of growth, and stay ahead of their competitors. For example, through predictive analytics, businesses can forecast future trends based on historical data, helping them plan more effectively.

In short, Business Intelligence equips companies with the tools they need to understand their past performance, assess their current operations, and make strategic decisions about the future. Whether you're running a small business or managing a global corporation, BI has the potential to drive growth, reduce inefficiencies, and open new opportunities.

By embracing BI, companies are no longer operating in the dark. They are using the power of data to illuminate the path forward.

## How Data Transforms into Actionable Insights

At its core, data is just raw information. Whether it's numbers in a spreadsheet, web traffic statistics, or customer reviews, data on its own doesn't hold much meaning. The real power of data emerges when it's analyzed and transformed into something more valuable: actionable insights. But how does that transformation happen?

**Step 1: Data Collection**

The first step in the process is data collection, and it's critical to get it right from the start. Businesses gather data from a wide range of sources—internal databases, sales records, customer interactions, and external sources like market research or social media. Each data source offers unique insights, but combining them provides a more comprehensive picture. It's like putting together pieces of a puzzle. Every piece you collect brings you closer to seeing the full image of your business performance.

**Step 2: Data Cleansing**

Once data is collected, the next step is to clean it. Raw data often contains errors—duplicates, incomplete records, or inconsistencies—that can distort your analysis. A common saying in business intelligence is "garbage in, garbage out." If you don't clean your data, any insights you derive from it will be unreliable. Cleansing involves removing errors, filling in missing information where possible, and ensuring that the data is consistent and standardized across all sources.

**Step 3: Data Analysis**

Now that your data is clean, it's ready to be analyzed. This is where data really starts to take shape. Various techniques, ranging from simple statistical analysis to advanced machine learning algorithms, are applied to uncover trends, patterns, and correlations. Imagine you own an e-commerce business and you want to understand why sales spike at certain times of the year. By analyzing your sales data, you might find that customer buying habits are closely tied to seasonal trends, and certain products perform better during specific months. This analysis helps you uncover hidden patterns that might not have been obvious just by looking at raw data.

**Step 4: Turning Data into Visuals**

Data analysis becomes even more powerful when it's visualized. Humans process visual information much more easily than rows of numbers in a spreadsheet. This is why business intelligence tools offer dashboards, charts, and graphs to help turn raw data into a visual story. For example, a line graph showing sales trends over time allows you to quickly spot spikes or dips, while a pie chart breaking down customer demographics helps you understand your audience at a glance. By using visuals, you make complex data more digestible, and more importantly, actionable.

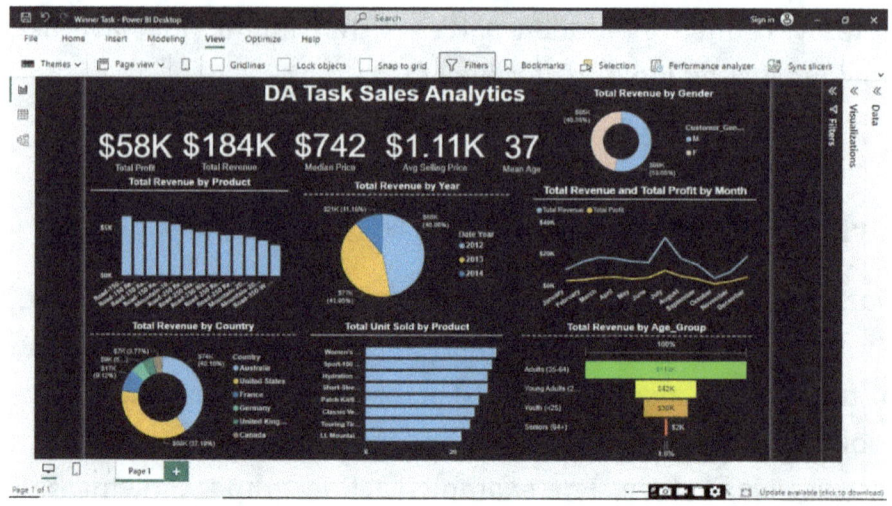

*Example of a Business Intelligence Dashboard showing Sales Trends and Customer Demographics. Source: Medium.*

### Step 5: Deriving Actionable Insights

The final step in the transformation process is converting your analysis into actionable insights. Data on its own doesn't help if you don't know what to do with it. After identifying trends or patterns, the next question should always be, "What can we do with this information?" For instance, if your sales data shows that a particular product consistently outperforms others during a specific season, you could plan to increase inventory before that season begins. Or, if customer feedback indicates dissatisfaction with a certain feature, you can prioritize product improvements. The key is to connect data insights directly to business actions that can drive improvements, whether it's boosting efficiency, increasing sales, or improving customer satisfaction.

**The Continuous Cycle**

It's important to note that the process of turning data into actionable insights is not a one-time event. It's a continuous cycle where data is constantly collected, cleansed, analyzed, and applied to new decisions. As your business grows and changes, so will the data, and the insights you can extract from it will evolve. The most successful companies make data analysis an ongoing part of their strategy, constantly refining their approach based on the latest information.

In this book, we'll dive deeper into each of these steps, showing you how to harness the full power of Business Intelligence to drive better decision-making. Whether you're new to data analytics or looking to refine your existing BI strategies, you'll find practical advice to help you transform data into your company's most valuable asset.

# Common Tools and Technologies

Business Intelligence relies heavily on specialized tools and technologies to collect, process, and visualize data. These tools simplify complex data sets, turning them into meaningful insights that help businesses make informed decisions. Whether you're a small business or a global enterprise, the right BI tools can streamline decision-making and unlock the potential hidden within your data. Let's look at some of the most common and powerful BI tools available today.

**Power BI**

Microsoft's Power BI is one of the most widely used BI tools. It offers a suite of analytics services that allow businesses to visualize their data through interactive dashboards and reports. One of the strengths of Power BI is its ability to connect to a wide variety of data sources, including spreadsheets, cloud-based services, and databases. Its intuitive drag-and-drop interface makes it user-friendly, even for those without a deep technical background. Power BI also integrates seamlessly with other Microsoft services like Excel and Azure, making it a convenient choice for organizations already using Microsoft products.

In addition to its core features, Power BI offers real-time analytics, allowing businesses to monitor live data and make decisions based on up-to-the-minute information. This makes it particularly useful for organizations that need to respond quickly to changing market conditions.

## Tableau

Tableau is another powerful tool that specializes in data visualization. It enables users to create a wide range of visuals, from simple graphs to complex, interactive dashboards, with minimal effort. One of Tableau's biggest selling points is its ability to process large amounts of data quickly, making it an excellent choice for businesses that need to analyze vast datasets.

Tableau is designed to be intuitive and easy to use, even for non-technical users, which is one of the reasons for its popularity. With drag-and-drop functionality and pre-built templates, it simplifies the process of turning raw data into compelling visuals. Additionally, Tableau's ability to integrate with numerous data sources, including databases, spreadsheets, and even cloud services, adds to its versatility.

## Google Analytics

For businesses focused on their digital presence, Google Analytics is an essential tool. It tracks and analyzes website traffic, providing detailed insights into how visitors interact with a website. This data helps businesses understand user behavior, track marketing campaigns, and identify areas for improvement on their site. Google Analytics offers a broad range of metrics, including page views, bounce rates, and conversion rates, which can be tailored to specific business goals.

What sets Google Analytics apart is its ability to provide real-time data and integrate with other Google services like Google Ads, making it a comprehensive tool for managing online marketing efforts.

**SAP BusinessObjects**

SAP BusinessObjects is a suite of front-end applications that help businesses manage data reporting and analysis. Known for its enterprise-level capabilities, SAP BusinessObjects is commonly used by large organizations that require robust, scalable BI solutions. The platform offers a variety of tools for reporting, visualization, and sharing data across different departments, ensuring that decision-makers have access to real-time insights.

SAP's strengths lie in its flexibility and customizability. It allows organizations to create highly tailored reports and dashboards that meet their unique business needs. Additionally, it integrates well with SAP's broader suite of enterprise solutions, making it a natural fit for companies already using SAP products.

**Qlik Sense**

Qlik Sense is another versatile BI tool that allows businesses to visualize data, create interactive reports, and explore data in depth. One of Qlik Sense's distinguishing features is its associative data model, which enables users to explore relationships within their data that might not be immediately apparent with traditional analysis methods. This model allows users to navigate freely through their data, following connections and trends that provide deeper insights.

Qlik Sense is designed to be accessible to users at all skill levels, offering self-service capabilities that let even non-technical users create their own reports and dashboards. It also supports collaboration, allowing teams to work together on data analysis in real time.

Each BI tool brings something unique to the table, whether it's Power BI's seamless integration with Microsoft services, Tableau's powerful visualizations, or Google Analytics' focus on digital marketing metrics. The right tool for your business will depend on your specific needs, the size of your organization, and the complexity of your data.

Chapter 2

# Implementing BI Strategies Across Business Functions

## Marketing with Data: Customer Insights and Trends

Data has transformed the way businesses approach marketing. Gone are the days when decisions were made solely on intuition or vague assumptions about what customers might want. Today, companies can tap into vast amounts of data to understand their customers on a much deeper level—helping them create more personalized, targeted, and effective marketing strategies.

**Understanding Your Customers Through Data**

Every interaction customers have with your brand—whether they browse your website, purchase a product, or leave a review—generates valuable data. But it's not just about collecting information. The key is turning that data into meaningful insights about who your customers are and what drives their behavior.

For example, by analyzing website traffic, social media activity, and purchase histories, you can identify important details about your customer base: their demographics, preferences, and buying patterns. Are they price-sensitive? Do they prefer shopping during sales, or do they tend to buy luxury items without waiting for discounts? These insights allow you to segment your audience into different groups, making it easier to target each group with tailored marketing efforts that are more likely to resonate with them.

**Predicting Trends and Behaviors**

Data isn't just about understanding what has already happened; it's also a powerful tool for predicting future trends. Predictive analytics allows businesses to anticipate customer behavior based on past data, helping marketers make smarter decisions.

Take, for instance, an online clothing retailer. By analyzing past sales, they might discover that certain products tend to spike in popularity during specific seasons or that a particular style becomes trendy in certain age groups. This information enables the retailer to stock the right inventory ahead of time and craft targeted marketing campaigns just before those trends emerge.

Similarly, data can help predict customer churn—the likelihood that a customer will stop engaging with your brand. By identifying patterns in customer behavior, such as a drop in interaction with marketing emails or fewer website visits, you can take proactive steps to re-engage those customers before they're gone for good.

**Personalization: The Secret to Engagement**

One of the most effective ways to use customer data is through personalization. Consumers today expect a personalized experience—generic, one-size-fits-all marketing no longer works in a world where each customer's preferences can be tracked and understood.

Think of Netflix or Spotify. These companies thrive on their ability to recommend content based on individual user behavior. The same principle applies to marketing. By tracking what customers buy, browse, and interact with, you can offer personalized recommendations that feel relevant and timely.

For example, if a customer regularly purchases athletic wear, sending them promotional emails for fitness gear rather than unrelated products increases the likelihood of engagement. This kind of personalized marketing not only boosts sales but also strengthens customer loyalty, as consumers are more likely to feel valued when they receive offers tailored specifically to their preferences.

*Example of Personalized Product Recommendations in Email Marketing. Source: shopagain.com.*

**Real-Time Insights for Better Decisions**

The beauty of modern data-driven marketing is that it provides real-time feedback, allowing businesses to adjust their strategies on the fly. With the right tools, marketers can track the performance of campaigns in real time, understanding which ads, emails, or social media posts are driving conversions and which ones are falling flat.

Let's say you launch a new email marketing campaign promoting a limited-time sale. By monitoring real-time data, you notice that the open rates are lower than expected. This immediate insight allows you to tweak the subject line or content of your emails to improve engagement, rather than waiting until the campaign is over to see results.

The ability to adapt in real time is crucial in today's fast-paced digital landscape. It allows marketers to stay agile, respond to changing customer needs, and maximize the effectiveness of their efforts without wasting time or resources.

**Using Data to Stay Ahead of Trends**

Data doesn't just help you react to current customer behavior, it also empowers you to stay ahead of emerging trends. By keeping an eye on broader market data—social media conversations, industry reports, and competitor activity—you can spot shifts in consumer preferences before they hit the mainstream.

For example, if you notice a growing number of conversations around sustainability in your industry, you could start emphasizing eco-friendly aspects of your products in your marketing campaigns. Being an early adopter of these trends not only positions your brand as forward-thinking but also gives you a competitive edge.

In this era, marketing without data is like navigating without a map. Data provides the insights necessary to understand your customers, predict their needs, and create personalized experiences that resonate. In the chapters to come, we'll explore more strategies on how to effectively integrate data into your marketing efforts and turn those insights into real-world success for your business.

## Financial Analytics: Optimizing Cost and Revenue

Financial analytics is one of the most valuable applications of BI, providing companies with the tools they need to make informed decisions about optimizing both costs and revenue. The goal of financial analytics is simple: to use data to create a clearer picture of a company's financial health and to identify opportunities to improve profitability. Whether it's managing expenses, increasing efficiency, or forecasting future revenues, BI helps businesses gain control over their financial performance and make strategic decisions that drive growth.

**Optimizing Costs with BI**

Managing costs is essential for maintaining profitability, and this is where BI tools truly shine. By collecting data from various departments, BI platforms can provide a detailed view of where money is being spent and whether those expenditures are delivering value. For example, through BI analysis, a company may discover inefficiencies in its supply chain, such as overstocking inventory or using high-cost suppliers when more affordable options are available. Identifying these issues in real time allows companies to take corrective actions before costs spiral out of control.

In addition to cutting down unnecessary expenses, BI also helps businesses forecast and allocate budgets more effectively. Historical data can be used to predict future costs, helping businesses allocate their resources more efficiently. For example, a manufacturing company can analyze seasonal trends in raw material prices and adjust its procurement strategy to purchase materials when prices are low, reducing overall costs.

BI tools also play a key role in labor cost optimization. Businesses can analyze workforce productivity data to determine how labor costs are affecting overall profitability. By identifying inefficiencies in staffing or scheduling, businesses can streamline operations without compromising service quality.

**Increasing Revenue with BI**

While cost optimization is critical, increasing revenue is equally important for sustaining growth. BI tools provide companies with the insights they need to identify new revenue opportunities, increase sales, and enhance customer relationships. One of the most powerful ways BI achieves this is by analyzing customer data.

Customer behavior patterns—such as purchasing habits, preferences, and feedback—can provide valuable insights into how to increase sales. By analyzing this data, businesses can personalize marketing efforts, optimize pricing strategies, and create targeted offers that resonate with specific customer segments. For instance, a retailer might use BI to track which products sell well together and develop promotions that bundle these items, driving up average transaction value.

BI also plays a crucial role in sales forecasting, helping businesses anticipate future revenue streams. By analyzing historical sales data alongside external factors like market trends and economic conditions, BI tools can help companies predict future demand. This allows businesses to adjust their production levels, stock inventory appropriately, and ensure that they're ready to meet customer needs at the right time.

In addition, BI helps businesses track their financial performance in real time, allowing them to quickly identify and respond to any issues affecting revenue. If sales are lower than expected in a particular region, BI tools can quickly highlight this trend, enabling businesses to take corrective actions such as launching targeted marketing campaigns or adjusting their product offerings.

**The Power of Predictive Analytics in Finance**

One of the most valuable features of BI in financial analytics is its predictive capabilities. Using historical data, BI tools can help businesses anticipate future financial trends and make data-driven decisions that support long-term financial health.

For example, a business might use predictive analytics to forecast its cash flow for the next quarter, helping it plan for potential shortfalls or surpluses. This foresight allows businesses to make strategic investments, cut costs where necessary, or prepare for potential financial challenges.

Predictive analytics also plays a critical role in risk management. By analyzing financial data and market conditions, businesses can identify potential risks to their revenue streams, such as economic downturns or changes in consumer behavior. This proactive approach allows companies to put contingency plans in place, protecting their revenue and profitability even in challenging conditions.

By combining cost optimization and revenue generation strategies with the power of BI, businesses can gain complete control over their financial health. The ability to analyze financial data in real time, forecast future trends, and make informed decisions based on data-driven insights is a game-changer for companies looking to thrive in today's competitive marketplace. Whether it's cutting down on unnecessary expenses or finding new ways to boost revenue, financial analytics powered by BI provides a roadmap for sustainable growth and profitability.

# Supply Chain and Operations Optimization

In today's fast-paced business environment, optimizing supply chains and operations is more critical than ever. Whether you're managing a small retail business or overseeing a global enterprise, an efficient supply chain can be the difference between thriving and struggling. With BI, companies can take a data-driven approach to streamline these processes, making them more efficient, cost-effective, and responsive to market changes.

**The Power of Data in Supply Chain Management**

Data plays a crucial role in supply chain optimization by providing insights into every aspect of the process—from sourcing raw materials to delivering finished products. Traditionally, businesses relied on experience and instinct to manage their operations. But with the rise of BI, companies now have access to real-time data that offers a comprehensive view of their supply chain. This allows them to identify bottlenecks, predict demand, and optimize inventory levels.

For example, a manufacturer can use BI tools to track the movement of goods from suppliers to warehouses and eventually to customers. If a delay is detected at any point, the system can alert the relevant teams, allowing them to adjust schedules, reroute shipments, or communicate with customers about potential delays. These real-time insights enable businesses to be more proactive, reducing the likelihood of costly disruptions.

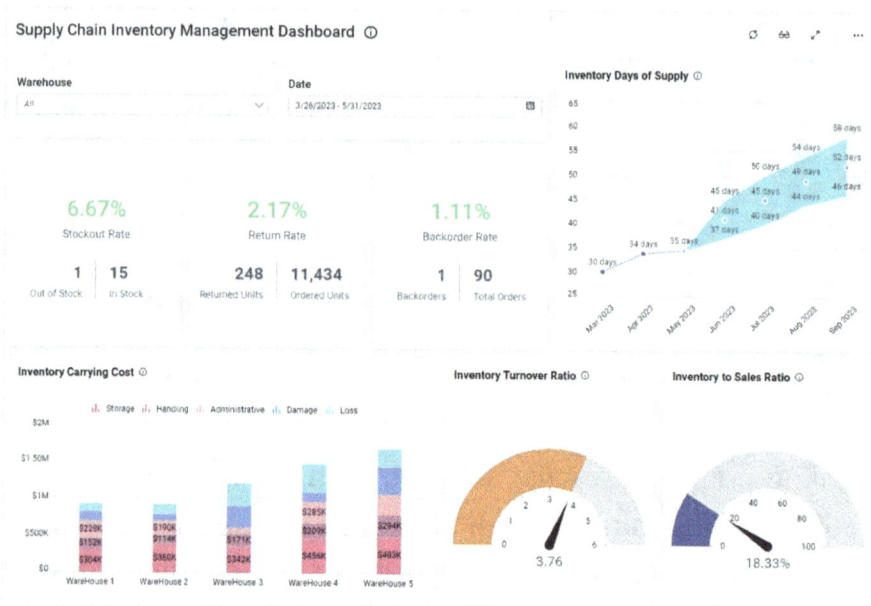

*Example of a Real-Time Supply Chain Dashboard Monitoring Inventory and Logistics. Source: boldbi.com*

## Predictive Analytics for Demand Forecasting

One of the most powerful applications of BI in supply chain management is predictive analytics. By analyzing historical data, businesses can forecast future demand with remarkable accuracy. This is especially useful in industries with fluctuating seasonal demand or unpredictable customer preferences.

Let's consider a retail company preparing for the holiday season. Instead of relying on guesswork or previous years' sales alone, they can use BI tools to analyze past sales trends, customer purchasing behavior, and even external factors like economic forecasts or weather patterns. Armed with this data, the company can adjust its inventory levels, ensuring they have the right amount of stock without over-ordering and tying up capital in excess inventory.

Predictive analytics also helps businesses anticipate potential supply chain disruptions. By analyzing data from suppliers, weather forecasts, or geopolitical events, companies can identify risks to their supply chain and develop contingency plans. For instance, if a major supplier is located in a region prone to natural disasters, the company can source backup suppliers in advance.

**Optimizing Operations for Efficiency**

Operations optimization is another area where BI can significantly enhance performance. Businesses generate vast amounts of operational data every day—machine performance, labor productivity, energy usage, and more. However, this data is often underutilized. By harnessing BI, companies can gain valuable insights into their operations and uncover opportunities for improvement.

For example, a manufacturing company might use BI to monitor the performance of its production lines. The system can track metrics such as machine downtime, production speed, and defect rates. If the data reveals that one machine is consistently causing delays due to maintenance issues, the company can schedule preventive maintenance before the problem escalates, avoiding costly production stoppages.

Another key area of operations optimization is workforce management. By analyzing employee performance data, businesses can identify trends in productivity and optimize shift schedules accordingly. For example, if data shows that certain teams are more productive during specific hours, management can adjust work shifts to capitalize on peak performance times, improving overall efficiency.

**Improving Inventory Management**

Inventory management is a delicate balancing act. Too much stock can tie up valuable capital and lead to waste, while too little can result in missed sales opportunities. BI tools allow businesses to manage inventory more effectively by providing real-time insights into stock levels, turnover rates, and replenishment needs.

Consider a business that relies on just-in-time (JIT) inventory management, where materials are ordered only when needed. BI tools can monitor inventory levels and automatically trigger orders when stock falls below a predefined threshold. This ensures that the business always has the right amount of inventory on hand, reducing storage costs and minimizing the risk of stockouts.

Additionally, BI can help businesses optimize their warehouse operations. By analyzing data on product movement and storage patterns, companies can redesign their warehouses for greater efficiency. For example, fast-moving items can be stored closer to the loading dock to minimize handling time, while slow-moving products can be placed in less accessible areas. This reduces the time and labor required to fulfill orders, improving overall operational efficiency.

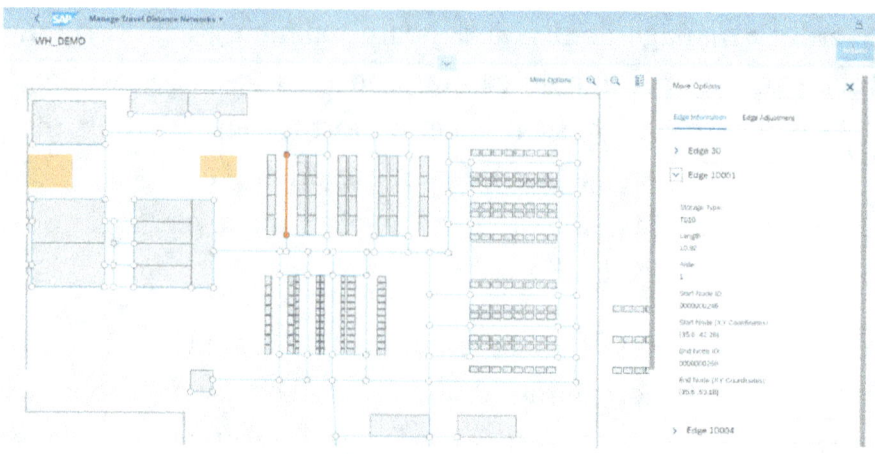

*Example of a Warehouse Layout Optimized with Data Insights (Manage Travel Distance Networks). Source: sap.com*

**Enhancing Collaboration Across the Supply Chain**

Supply chains involve multiple stakeholders—suppliers, manufacturers, distributors, and retailers—each playing a critical role in ensuring products reach customers efficiently. BI can enhance collaboration across these different stakeholders by providing a single source of truth. When all parties have access to the same data, communication becomes more transparent, and decisions can be made more quickly.

For example, a retailer can share demand forecasts with its suppliers, allowing them to adjust production schedules accordingly. Similarly, distributors can use BI tools to optimize delivery routes, reducing fuel costs and improving delivery times. This level of collaboration ensures that the entire supply chain operates more smoothly and efficiently, benefiting everyone involved.

**Building an Agile and Resilient Supply Chain**

The COVID-19 pandemic showed the importance of having a flexible and resilient supply chain. Many businesses faced severe disruptions due to factory shutdowns, transportation delays, and unpredictable demand spikes. Companies that had already embraced BI were better positioned to adapt quickly. They could use real-time data to identify alternative suppliers, shift production to different locations, and adjust their inventory levels to meet changing demand.

In a world where disruptions can come from anywhere—natural disasters, political unrest, or global pandemics—having an agile supply chain is crucial. BI gives businesses the tools they need to respond to these challenges, ensuring they remain competitive and resilient in an uncertain market.

With BI, supply chain and operations optimization is no longer about reacting to problems as they arise. It's about using data proactively to make informed decisions, improving efficiency, and staying ahead of the competition.

Chapter 3

# Data-Driven Leadership and Decision Making

## The Role of Executives in a BI-Driven Business

In a BI-driven business, executives play a pivotal role in ensuring that data-driven decision-making becomes an integral part of the company's culture and operations. While BI provides powerful tools and insights, its effectiveness largely depends on how leaders integrate those insights into strategic decisions. The role of an executive goes beyond approving BI tools; it requires actively fostering a data-driven mindset throughout the organization and ensuring that every team understands the value of leveraging BI to achieve business objectives.

**Championing a Data-Driven Culture**

One of the most important responsibilities for executives is to champion a data-driven culture. This means creating an environment where decisions are made based on data, not just intuition or past practices. When executives prioritize data over opinion, it sets an example for the rest of the organization. Leaders who encourage teams to base their decisions on BI insights will see those teams become more aligned with the company's strategic goals. This kind of cultural shift starts at the top and requires consistent reinforcement. Executives need to regularly communicate the importance of data-driven decision-making in meetings, company updates, and strategic discussions.

Moreover, fostering a culture that embraces BI requires more than just words; it demands investment in both the technology and the people who will use it. Executives need to ensure that the right BI tools are available to employees and that staff receive adequate training to make the most of these tools. When employees are confident in their ability to use data to inform their decisions, they are more likely to adopt and embrace the systems that executives have put in place.

**Strategic Decision-Making with BI**

At the executive level, the stakes of decision-making are often high. Decisions related to investments, market expansions, and mergers can have long-term implications for a business's future. BI empowers executives to make informed decisions by providing them with real-time, accurate data that highlights market trends, customer behavior, and operational performance.

For example, when considering a new market entry, executives can use BI to analyze potential demand, competitive landscape, and the costs associated with entering that market. Instead of relying on gut feeling, they have access to concrete data that reveals both opportunities and risks. This allows them to create more precise strategies and better allocate resources.

Furthermore, BI can help executives spot trends before they fully develop, giving the business a competitive advantage. In a BI-driven business, executives who consistently rely on data to shape their strategies are more agile, better prepared for market changes, and able to anticipate customer needs before their competitors do.

**Bridging the Gap Between Data and Action**

While BI generates valuable insights, it's the responsibility of executives to bridge the gap between those insights and actionable strategies. It's not enough to receive reports; executives must work closely with their teams to translate BI findings into measurable actions. This often involves setting clear priorities, allocating resources effectively, and ensuring that every part of the organization is aligned with the overall strategy.

For instance, if BI reveals inefficiencies in the supply chain, it's up to executives to coordinate with operations teams, procurement, and logistics to address the problem. They need to ask the right questions: How can we streamline our processes? What resources do we need to improve performance? How can we use this data to make long-term improvements? The ability to turn data into action is what sets effective leaders apart in a BI-driven business.

**Building Trust in Data**

For BI to truly drive a business forward, executives need to build trust in the data. This starts with ensuring the quality and accuracy of the information that's being used. Executives must invest in the right data governance policies to ensure that data is clean, accurate, and up-to-date. They also need to encourage transparency in how data is collected and shared across departments.

Trust in data also extends to decision-making processes. When employees see that their leaders are using data to make informed decisions, it builds confidence in the system and encourages wider adoption of BI tools. Executives should frequently showcase the impact of data-driven decisions on company performance, reinforcing the importance of BI across all levels of the organization.

In summary, the role of executives in a BI-driven business is multifaceted. They are not just decision-makers but champions of data-driven culture, strategic thinkers who rely on BI insights, and catalysts for turning data into action. By fully embracing BI, executives can lead their companies to be more agile, efficient, and prepared for future challenges.

# Strategic BI Use in High-Stakes Decision-Making

When the stakes are high, business decisions require more than intuition or past experience—they need data-driven precision. Whether it's deciding to expand into new markets, launching a new product, or navigating a merger, these decisions can shape the future of an organization. This is where BI steps in, offering leaders the tools to make informed, strategic choices with confidence.

### Data as a Decision-Making Powerhouse

At the heart of every high-stakes decision is uncertainty. What if the expansion fails? What if a new product doesn't meet market demand? BI helps reduce that uncertainty by providing deep insights into the factors driving these crucial decisions.

Through the analysis of historical data, market trends, and predictive models, executives can anticipate potential outcomes, weigh risks, and identify opportunities that would otherwise be missed.

For example, a company considering expanding into an international market can use BI to analyze customer behavior in that region, assess competitor presence, and predict the financial impact of entering a new market. BI tools can map out various scenarios, allowing leaders to visualize the potential risks and rewards associated with each choice.

**Real-Time Data for Agile Decision-Making**

The business landscape can change quickly, especially during high-stakes situations like mergers or acquisitions. In these moments, having access to real-time data is invaluable. BI systems provide continuous updates on key performance indicators (KPIs), market movements, and internal metrics, allowing decision-makers to adjust their strategies on the fly.

Imagine a company undergoing a merger with a competitor. As financials, customer data, and operational processes are integrated, executives need real-time updates to monitor progress and respond to any emerging challenges. BI tools can offer insights into how well the two companies are aligning, identify areas where processes are falling behind, and ensure that the integration stays on track.

This real-time access to information not only improves decision-making but also provides leaders with the flexibility to pivot their strategies if the data reveals unexpected trends or issues.

## Risk Management with Predictive Analytics

One of the most significant advantages of using BI in high-stakes decision-making is its ability to manage risk. Predictive analytics allows companies to simulate different outcomes and assess the likelihood of success or failure before committing to a course of action.

For instance, when launching a new product, companies can use BI tools to analyze past product launches, customer preferences, and market conditions to forecast demand. Predictive models can reveal whether the product will likely succeed, how much inventory is needed, and what pricing strategy would be optimal. By simulating these scenarios, companies can mitigate risks and avoid costly mistakes.

## BI and Strategic Flexibility

In high-stakes situations, adaptability is crucial. BI enables businesses to remain agile by providing actionable insights that guide their next moves. Take the case of a company facing an economic downturn. Using BI, leadership can identify the most vulnerable areas of their operations, such as declining sales in a particular region or increased supply chain costs.

With this information, they can take proactive measures—cutting unnecessary expenses, reallocating resources to more profitable areas, or re-negotiating supplier contracts. Instead of making reactionary cuts across the board, they can make targeted, strategic adjustments that ensure long-term stability without sacrificing growth.

**Building Confidence in Complex Decisions**

Executives often face complex, multi-faceted decisions with far-reaching consequences. Whether it's deciding which market to enter, how to structure a new business unit, or when to invest in emerging technologies, these decisions come with high pressure. BI provides clarity amidst this complexity by breaking down vast amounts of data into understandable insights that can inform these decisions.

With BI, executives don't just make decisions—they make confident decisions backed by data. The ability to visualize possible outcomes, assess risks, and evaluate real-time data allows business leaders to move forward with assurance, knowing they are making well-informed choices that align with their company's strategic objectives.

In high-stakes decision-making, where every choice can dramatically impact the future of an organization, BI transforms uncertainty into opportunity. By leveraging data-driven insights, leaders can navigate even the most complex decisions with precision and confidence.

## Challenges in Shifting to Data-Driven Leadership

Shifting from traditional leadership models to a data-driven approach comes with a unique set of challenges. While the benefits of data-driven decision-making are widely recognized, making the transition is not always smooth. Executives and leaders must navigate several hurdles, including cultural resistance, technical complexity, and the need for new skills. These challenges can slow the adoption of BI, but understanding and addressing them head-on can help leaders guide their organizations through the transition more effectively.

**Resistance to Change**

One of the most common challenges in shifting to data-driven leadership is resistance to change. Many organizations have relied on gut instincts, personal experience, or established procedures for years. When leaders suddenly introduce BI tools and analytics, it can feel threatening to teams and even senior management. Employees may be concerned that their decision-making authority will be undermined by data, or they might worry that they'll need to acquire new skills to remain relevant.

The key to overcoming this resistance is communication and education. Leaders need to make it clear that BI is a tool designed to enhance decision-making, not replace human judgment. It's important to show how data can support better choices, leading to improved outcomes for the business as a whole. Additionally, providing ongoing training can help employees feel more comfortable using new BI tools and reduce anxiety about learning new technologies.

**Overcoming Silos and Fragmented Data**

Data silos are another significant challenge when shifting to a data-driven leadership model. Many businesses operate with fragmented systems, where different departments use separate tools and databases that don't communicate with each other.

This leads to data being trapped in isolated silos, making it difficult to get a comprehensive view of the business.

For example, the sales department might track customer data in one system, while the marketing team uses a different platform. Without integration, it becomes nearly impossible for leaders to analyze data holistically. This can result in missed opportunities and inefficient operations.

Breaking down these silos requires a coordinated effort. Leaders must prioritize data integration across departments, ensuring that all teams are working with a unified system. Implementing cross-functional BI tools that pull data from multiple sources into one central platform can help create a seamless flow of information. This not only improves decision-making but also fosters collaboration across departments.

**Building Trust in Data**

Another significant challenge is building trust in the data itself. Leaders may be skeptical of the insights they receive if the data is incomplete, inconsistent, or inaccurate. This skepticism can undermine the transition to a data-driven culture and cause hesitation in using BI tools for critical decisions.

Ensuring data accuracy and reliability is crucial to building this trust. Companies must establish strong data governance policies that define how data is collected, stored, and maintained. Regular audits of data quality should be performed, and clear standards must be set to ensure that the information executives are using is valid and trustworthy.

It's also important to make data transparent and accessible to everyone in the organization. When employees at all levels have access to the same data, it fosters a sense of accountability and trust. Leaders can demonstrate how data is being used effectively, further building confidence in its accuracy.

**Adapting to New Decision-Making Models**

Data-driven leadership often requires a shift in how decisions are made. Traditionally, many organizations have relied on hierarchical decision-making processes where senior leaders make top-down choices based on their experience. However, BI encourages a more collaborative and decentralized approach, where decisions are driven by data insights and supported by various teams.

This change can be challenging for leaders who are used to having the final say without input from data or lower-level teams. It requires a mindset shift, where leaders are open to allowing data to challenge assumptions and influence decisions.

While experience and intuition still play a role, data should guide strategy.

To make this transition, leaders need to encourage a culture of open dialogue around data. Teams should feel empowered to present data-driven insights to inform key decisions, and leaders must be willing to listen. This helps create a balanced decision-making model where both data and human insight are valued.

**The Learning Curve for BI Tools**

Adopting BI tools can come with a steep learning curve, especially for leaders who have not worked closely with data analytics before. The complexity of some BI platforms, combined with the need to interpret large amounts of data, can be overwhelming. Executives may feel unequipped to lead in this new environment if they are not confident in their ability to use BI tools effectively.

Investing in continuous education is essential to overcome this hurdle. Leaders should not only familiarize themselves with the BI tools their organization uses but also understand the fundamentals of data analysis. Training programs, workshops, and collaboration with data specialists can help bridge this knowledge gap. As executives become more comfortable interpreting data, they will be better equipped to lead a BI-driven organization with confidence.

Transitioning to a data-driven leadership model is not without its challenges, but overcoming these obstacles is essential for businesses looking to thrive in an increasingly competitive and data-centric world. When leaders address these issues—resistance to change, data silos, building trust in data, adapting decision-making models, and overcoming the learning curve—they pave the way for a smoother, more successful integration of BI into their business operations.

Chapter 4

# Real-World Case Studies in Business Intelligence

## Small Businesses Using BI to Grow

Many small business owners might think that BI is only for large corporations with vast resources. However, that's far from the truth. In fact, small businesses stand to gain significantly from using BI, often turning it into their secret weapon for growth. By leveraging data-driven insights, small businesses can compete more effectively, make smarter decisions, and scale efficiently—without the guesswork that often limits growth.

**Understanding Customers Better**

For any business, understanding the customer is key to growth, and small businesses are no exception. BI tools allow even the smallest companies to dive deep into customer behavior, identifying trends and preferences that might not be immediately obvious. A small e-commerce shop, for instance, can track which products are most popular at specific times, identify which marketing campaigns are driving the most sales, and even analyze what types of customers are most loyal.

With this kind of insight, small businesses can create personalized marketing strategies, send more targeted promotions, and adjust inventory to better meet customer demand. It's not about outspending competitors on marketing—it's about being smarter with the data at hand.

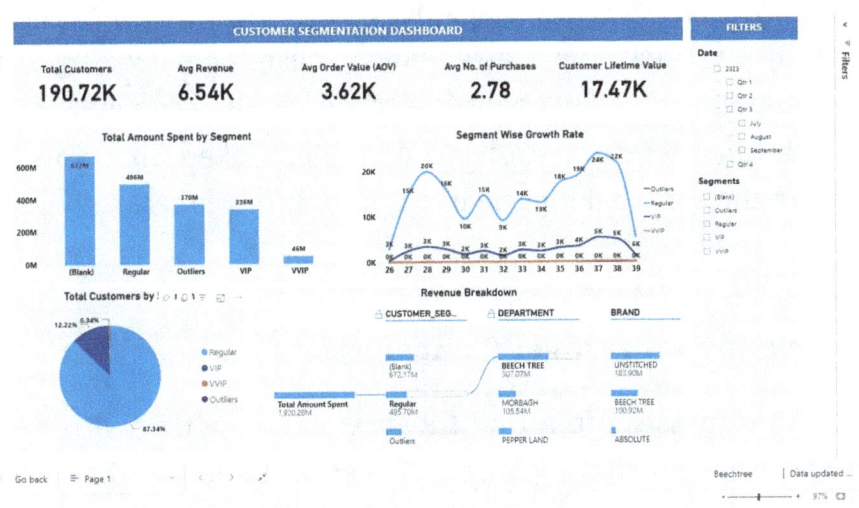

*Example of a Customer Segmentation Dashboard. Source: reddit.com*

## Improving Operational Efficiency

Efficiency is critical for small businesses that often operate on tight budgets. BI tools help owners and managers optimize day-to-day operations by providing real-time insights into how different areas of the business are performing. For example, a small bakery might use BI to monitor inventory levels, ensuring they don't over-order ingredients while still keeping enough stock to meet demand. This reduces waste, saves money, and allows the business to operate more smoothly.

Similarly, a service-based business like a local fitness studio can use BI to track class attendance, customer bookings, and cancellation rates. By analyzing this data, they can adjust class schedules, offer promotions to fill underbooked time slots, and ensure they are making the most of their resources.

**Competing with Larger Companies**

Small businesses often find themselves competing with larger, more established companies. However, BI levels the playing field. With access to the same powerful data insights, small businesses can make decisions just as strategic and data-informed as their larger competitors.

For example, a small boutique might use BI to track not only its own sales but also monitor broader market trends. By analyzing public data, like fashion trends or consumer spending patterns, the boutique can stock up on popular items just before they become mainstream, ensuring they stay ahead of larger competitors who might be slower to react.

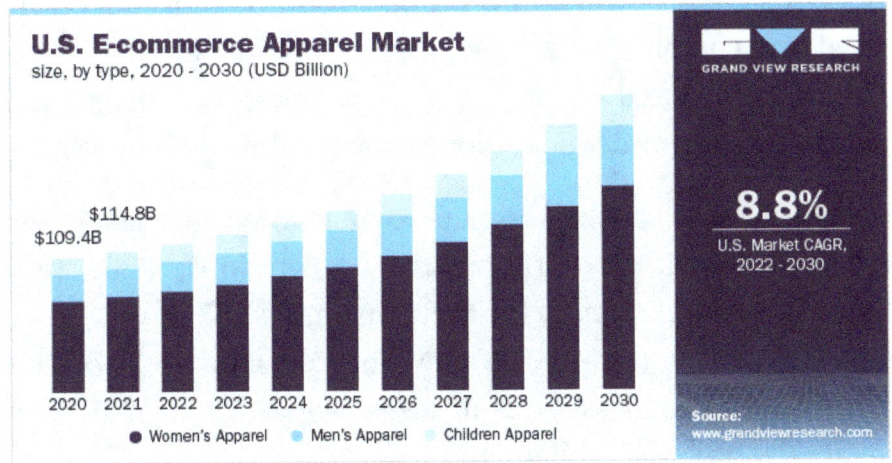

E-commerce Apparel Market Size. Source: grandviewresearch.com

## Driving Growth with Data

One of the most powerful aspects of BI for small businesses is its ability to guide growth strategies. Let's say a local coffee shop wants to expand by opening a second location. Rather than relying on gut feelings about where the new shop should be located, the owners can use BI to analyze foot traffic data, local demographics, and competitors' locations. This kind of data-driven decision-making reduces the risk of opening in the wrong area, ensuring the new location has the best chance of success.

Similarly, a small business looking to expand its product line can use BI to predict which new products will be most successful based on customer purchase history and emerging trends. Instead of trial and error, BI gives businesses the insight they need to make confident decisions about where and how to grow.

BI offers small businesses the opportunity to make more informed decisions, optimize their operations, and create personalized experiences for their customers. What was once a tool for large enterprises is now an accessible and powerful resource for businesses of all sizes, allowing them to grow smarter, faster, and with greater confidence.

## Global Enterprises Thriving with BI

In the fast-paced global business landscape, some of the world's largest companies have mastered the art of using BI to stay ahead of the competition. These enterprises have not only adopted BI but have embedded it into the core of their decision-making processes. BI helps these companies make sense of vast amounts of data, uncovering insights that inform their strategies, streamline operations, and ultimately drive growth.

## Amazon: Data-Driven from the Start

Amazon is perhaps one of the most famous examples of a company that thrives on data. From its inception, Amazon has used BI to optimize its operations, refine customer experiences, and expand into new markets. The company's recommendation engine, powered by sophisticated BI algorithms, analyzes user behavior to suggest products, increasing customer engagement and sales. This data-driven approach ensures that Amazon stays ahead by continuously evolving with customer preferences and market trends.

Beyond recommendations, Amazon also uses BI to optimize its supply chain and logistics. The company processes vast amounts of real-time data to forecast demand, optimize inventory management, and improve delivery times. This allows Amazon to run one of the most efficient supply chains in the world, enabling it to deliver goods faster and at lower costs.

## Netflix: Personalizing Content with Data

Netflix is another global giant that has successfully integrated BI into its core business strategy. The company's ability to analyze viewer data in real time allows it to offer personalized content recommendations, keeping users engaged for longer periods. Every time a user watches a show, pauses a movie, or rates a series, Netflix captures that data to refine its algorithms.

Netflix doesn't just stop at recommendations. The company also uses BI to make content creation decisions. By analyzing viewing habits, Netflix can predict which genres, actors, or storylines will resonate most with its audience. This data-driven approach to content creation has allowed Netflix to produce hits like *Stranger Things* and *The Crown*, ensuring its continued success in a competitive streaming market.

**Coca-Cola: Streamlining Operations with BI**

Coca-Cola, one of the world's most recognized brands, also harnesses the power of BI to streamline its global operations. With a presence in more than 200 countries, Coca-Cola must manage complex supply chains, track sales performance, and monitor consumer preferences across a wide range of markets. BI allows the company to track these metrics in real time, ensuring it stays agile and responsive to market demands.

For instance, Coca-Cola uses data analytics to optimize its production processes. By analyzing sales data and consumer behavior, the company can predict demand and adjust production schedules accordingly, ensuring they always have the right amount of product available in different regions. This reduces waste and improves efficiency, saving costs while meeting customer needs more effectively.

**Walmart: Staying Competitive with Real-Time Data**

Walmart, the world's largest retailer, is another excellent example of a company thriving on BI. The company processes an enormous amount of transactional data daily, using it to make real-time decisions on everything from inventory management to pricing strategies. Walmart's use of data allows it to forecast demand accurately, ensuring that products are always in stock while minimizing excess inventory.

BI also helps Walmart stay competitive in its pricing strategy. The company monitors competitor pricing and adjusts its own in real time, ensuring that it consistently offers the best value to customers. Additionally, Walmart leverages BI to analyze shopping patterns, allowing it to optimize store layouts, enhance the customer experience, and drive more sales.

Global enterprises like Amazon, Netflix, Coca-Cola, and Walmart demonstrate the transformative power of BI. By embedding data into their decision-making processes, these companies have gained a competitive edge, allowing them to adapt quickly to market changes, optimize operations, and deliver exceptional value to customers. BI is not just a tool; it is a key driver of growth and innovation in today's global business environment.

## Lessons Learned from BI Failures

Business Intelligence can be a game changer for organizations—when implemented successfully. However, not all BI initiatives go according to plan. Many businesses have experienced BI failures, often leading to wasted resources, unmet goals, and internal frustrations. But failures aren't entirely negative—they offer valuable lessons that can guide future success.

**Poor Data Quality Leads to Poor Outcomes**

One of the most common reasons for BI failure is poor data quality. Companies might rush to implement BI tools without ensuring the accuracy and consistency of their data. When the foundation of BI is faulty, the insights drawn from it will be unreliable. For instance, if a company's data is full of duplicates, missing entries, or outdated information, BI systems will generate inaccurate reports. Decision-makers might act on this flawed data, leading to poor business outcomes.

The lesson here is simple: **good data equals good insights.** Ensuring your data is clean, complete, and consistent is critical before implementing any BI system. Regular data audits and cleansing processes are essential to maintaining this quality.

**Lack of User Adoption**

Even the most powerful BI tools are worthless if employees aren't using them. A major reason for BI failure is a lack of user adoption. Companies often invest in BI software without properly training their teams or integrating the system into daily operations. When employees don't understand how to use the tools, or when they don't see the value in using them, adoption rates plummet, and the BI system falls into disuse.

The takeaway here is the importance of **training and engagement**. It's not enough to simply implement a BI system—you need to actively involve your employees, show them how it benefits their work, and provide ongoing support to ensure the system is used effectively. User-friendly interfaces and strong leadership support can also drive adoption.

**Misalignment with Business Goals**

Another major cause of BI failure is when the system isn't aligned with the company's business goals. Sometimes, companies implement BI without clearly defining what they hope to achieve. They might gather data and generate reports but fail to connect those insights to tangible business outcomes. BI is a tool meant to serve specific goals, whether it's improving sales, reducing costs, or optimizing operations. Without this clear direction, businesses may find themselves drowning in data without knowing how to use it.

The lesson? **Align BI with your objectives.** Before launching a BI initiative, ensure you have well-defined business goals and that the system is built to provide insights that directly support those goals. Every report generated should lead to actionable insights that help the company meet its objectives.

### Overcomplicating the System

Some businesses make the mistake of overcomplicating their BI systems. They try to track too many metrics or use overly complex dashboards that overwhelm users. This complexity often results in confusion rather than clarity, with decision-makers unsure of what the data is telling them. Simplicity is key to ensuring BI delivers clear, actionable insights.

The lesson here is to **keep it simple**. Focus on tracking key performance indicators (KPIs) that are directly relevant to your business goals. Ensure that your BI dashboards are easy to navigate and that users can quickly interpret the data. Complexity doesn't equal sophistication—clarity and usability are far more valuable.

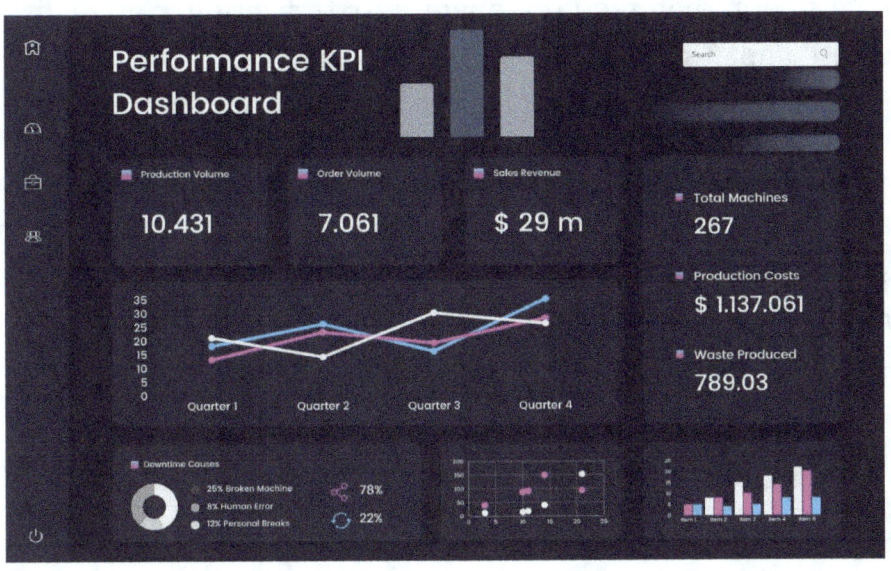

*Example of a Simplified Dashboard Showing Key Metrics. Source: b-cdn.net*

**Unrealistic Expectations**

Sometimes, companies approach BI with unrealistic expectations, believing it will solve all their problems overnight. BI is a powerful tool, but it doesn't offer instant results. Implementing BI requires time, effort, and strategic planning. Companies that expect quick fixes often end up disappointed when the system doesn't immediately deliver.

The takeaway is to **manage expectations**. BI is a long-term investment that requires ongoing optimization. Set realistic goals and timelines, and understand that BI will offer incremental improvements rather than instant transformations.

BI failures often stem from poor data quality, lack of user adoption, misalignment with business goals, overcomplicating systems, and unrealistic expectations. By learning from these mistakes, businesses can build more robust, effective BI strategies that drive real growth and improvement.

Chapter 5

# Overcoming Common BI Challenges

## Breaking Down Data Silos for Seamless Integration

One of the biggest obstacles businesses face when adopting BI is the issue of data silos. A data silo occurs when information is isolated within a specific department or system, making it difficult for other parts of the organization to access or utilize that data. In a siloed environment, each department operates independently, often with its own tools and databases. While this may seem manageable in the short term, it can cause inefficiencies, slow decision-making, and lead to missed opportunities. Breaking down these silos and creating a seamless integration of data across the organization is crucial for the success of any BI initiative.

**Understanding the Problem with Data Silos**

When data is locked away in silos, it hinders the flow of information. Departments may be sitting on valuable insights that could benefit other teams, but those insights never make it across the organization. For example, the marketing team might have customer insights that could help the product development team better understand user preferences, but if their systems aren't connected, this valuable information may never reach the people who need it most.

This lack of integration can lead to decisions being made based on incomplete or outdated data, creating a disconnect between different parts of the business. As a result, companies might miss opportunities to optimize their processes, improve customer satisfaction, or innovate new products. The longer silos persist, the more fragmented the company's overall strategy becomes, which is why breaking them down is critical.

**Creating a Unified Data Infrastructure**

The key to overcoming data silos is creating a unified data infrastructure where information flows freely between departments. This involves integrating different systems, tools, and databases so that all data can be accessed and analyzed in one central platform.

For instance, many organizations use a combination of customer relationship management (CRM) software, enterprise resource planning (ERP) systems, and marketing automation platforms. By connecting these systems through an integrated BI platform, businesses can pull data from multiple sources into a single dashboard. This allows for a more comprehensive view of the company's performance, as teams can analyze data from different departments side by side.

A unified infrastructure also ensures that data is consistent across the organization. If one department updates customer information, that change should be reflected in every system, eliminating discrepancies and ensuring that all teams are working with the most up-to-date data.

**Encouraging Cross-Departmental Collaboration**

Breaking down data silos isn't just a technical challenge, it's also a cultural one. In many organizations, departments operate in silos because they've grown accustomed to working independently. Teams might be reluctant to share data due to concerns about data ownership, accountability, or a lack of trust in how other departments will use the information.

To address this, leaders need to foster a culture of collaboration, where data is viewed as a shared resource that benefits the entire company. One way to encourage this shift is by setting up cross-departmental teams to work on key projects. For example, a team made up of members from marketing, sales, and product development can work together to analyze customer data, share insights, and create strategies that benefit all departments.

Leaders can also set clear expectations around data sharing and collaboration, ensuring that every team understands the importance of breaking down silos. When departments see the positive impact of shared data, they are more likely to embrace the idea of working together.

**Leveraging Cloud-Based Solutions for Seamless Integration**

Cloud-based BI solutions can play a pivotal role in breaking down data silos. Unlike traditional on-premise systems, cloud-based platforms allow for easy data integration and real-time collaboration. Teams from different locations or departments can access and analyze data simultaneously, enabling more dynamic and agile decision-making.

Cloud platforms also make it easier to scale data integration efforts. As your business grows and adopts new tools, cloud-based BI systems can quickly integrate these new data sources without the need for complex, time-consuming updates. This flexibility ensures that businesses can continue breaking down silos as they evolve, maintaining a seamless flow of information across the organization.

By leveraging cloud-based BI tools, companies can make their data more accessible, enabling teams to collaborate effectively and make informed decisions based on a unified view of the business.

Breaking down data silos is essential for any organization looking to thrive with BI. By creating a unified data infrastructure, fostering cross-departmental collaboration, and leveraging cloud-based solutions, businesses can ensure that data flows freely, empowering every part of the organization to make informed, data-driven decisions.

## Ensuring Data Quality and Accuracy

Data quality is the backbone of effective BI. No matter how sophisticated your BI tools are, if the data feeding into them is flawed, the insights you extract will be unreliable. Ensuring data quality and accuracy is not just a technical task, it's a foundational part of making sure your decisions are based on trustworthy information.

**Why Data Quality Matters**

Poor data quality can have serious consequences for a business. Imagine a company using customer data to target marketing campaigns. If the data contains errors like outdated contact information or duplicated entries, marketing efforts could be wasted, leading to missed opportunities and lost revenue. Even worse, when leaders rely on inaccurate data to make high-level decisions, the entire organization can be steered in the wrong direction.

High-quality data ensures that decisions are based on the right facts, making your BI tools not just more effective, but also more valuable to the organization.

**Key Components of Data Quality**

Data quality doesn't just refer to whether information is correct. It encompasses several factors that all contribute to ensuring accuracy and reliability:

1. **Accuracy**: The data must be correct and free of errors. For example, customer addresses must be up-to-date, and financial records should reflect the correct transactions.

2. **Completeness**: Incomplete data can skew analysis. For instance, missing customer purchase history might lead to flawed conclusions about buying habits.

3. **Consistency**: Data should be consistent across all systems and sources. If one system says a customer's name is "John Doe" while another lists it as "Johnathan Doe," that inconsistency can create confusion and disrupt analysis.

4. **Timeliness**: Data needs to be current. Outdated data can lead to poor decisions, especially in fast-moving industries like retail or finance.

5. **Relevance**: Data should be relevant to the business goals. Storing and analyzing data that doesn't directly contribute to decision-making can waste time and resources.

**Steps to Ensure Data Quality**

Ensuring data quality is an ongoing process that requires regular attention and maintenance. Here are the most effective strategies for maintaining high data quality:

**1. Implement Data Governance Policies**

Data governance refers to the policies and procedures that ensure data is managed and maintained properly across an organization. By establishing clear data governance rules, businesses can standardize how data is collected, stored, and processed. This reduces the likelihood of errors creeping into the system and ensures that data quality remains high over time.

For example, a retail company might enforce policies that require all customer information to be verified before it's entered into the system. This simple step can significantly reduce errors and improve data quality.

## 2. Regular Data Audits

Performing regular data audits is essential to maintaining accuracy. These audits help identify any issues with data consistency, accuracy, or completeness. By systematically reviewing the data, businesses can catch and correct errors before they affect decision-making.

A good audit process might involve checking data across multiple systems for consistency. If one system shows a different value than another, you know there's a discrepancy that needs addressing.

## 3. Data Cleansing

Data cleansing is the process of correcting or removing incorrect, incomplete, or outdated information from your database. This might involve eliminating duplicate entries, filling in missing information, or updating outdated records.

For instance, a company might run a cleansing process on its customer database to remove duplicate records or update phone numbers and email addresses that are no longer in use. This helps maintain a clean, usable data set that supports better analysis.

**4. Continuous Monitoring**

Even with governance and audits in place, data can degrade over time. That's why it's important to continuously monitor the quality of your data. BI tools often have built-in functionality that allows for real-time data quality monitoring, flagging potential issues before they become larger problems.

For example, a logistics company might use BI to monitor its delivery data. If the system detects that delivery times are being reported inconsistently, it can alert the team to investigate and correct the issue immediately.

**The Role of Automation in Data Quality**

Automation plays an increasingly important role in ensuring data quality. Many BI tools now offer automated data cleansing, validation, and auditing features that make it easier to maintain high standards. By automating these tasks, businesses can reduce human error, save time, and ensure more consistent data quality over time.

For instance, an e-commerce business might use automated tools to regularly cleanse its customer data, removing inactive accounts and updating customer preferences based on recent interactions. This ensures the data feeding into BI systems remains current and accurate, leading to better-targeted marketing campaigns and improved customer engagement.

In BI, data quality is not just a technical requirement, it's a business necessity. Ensuring that data is accurate, complete, consistent, and relevant is crucial to making decisions that drive success. Businesses that invest in data quality are better positioned to extract actionable insights, make informed decisions, and gain a competitive edge in their industry.

## Managing Data Privacy and Ethical Concerns

As businesses become more data-driven, managing data privacy and addressing ethical concerns are becoming increasingly important. Companies that collect and analyze data face growing scrutiny from both regulators and the public about how that data is used, stored, and protected. In this section, we'll explore the challenges of data privacy and ethics in the context of BI and provide insight into how companies can navigate these concerns responsibly.

## Protecting Customer Data in the Age of BI

One of the biggest responsibilities businesses face when using BI is ensuring the privacy of customer data. Today's BI systems are capable of processing vast amounts of personal information, from purchasing habits to geographic locations and browsing behavior. While this data is invaluable for making informed decisions, it comes with the responsibility to safeguard it.

Businesses must take steps to protect customer data from unauthorized access or breaches. This means employing robust security measures like encryption, multi-factor authentication, and regular audits of their systems. Additionally, companies must comply with data protection regulations such as the General Data Protection Regulation (GDPR) in Europe or the California Consumer Privacy Act (CCPA) in the United States. These laws give consumers more control over their personal data, and failure to comply can result in hefty fines or reputational damage.

Beyond compliance, businesses need to be transparent with customers about how their data is being used. Clearly communicating data policies and giving users the option to control their own information can build trust and demonstrate a commitment to ethical data use.

**Navigating Ethical Considerations**

While privacy laws dictate how data must be handled, ethical concerns go beyond legal compliance. Companies must also consider how they use data to avoid unethical practices or unintended harm. One area where this becomes particularly important is in the use of algorithms. BI tools often rely on machine learning algorithms to predict trends, identify patterns, and even make recommendations. However, algorithms are only as good as the data they are trained on, and biased or incomplete data can lead to unfair or discriminatory outcomes.

For example, an algorithm used by a bank to predict creditworthiness might inadvertently favor certain demographics if the training data reflects historical biases. Similarly, a retailer using BI to personalize marketing might unintentionally exclude specific customer segments if their data is not well represented in the analysis. Ethical data use requires careful consideration of how algorithms are developed, tested, and applied to ensure they don't perpetuate inequality or harm vulnerable groups.

To manage these concerns, companies should establish clear ethical guidelines for data use, ensuring that diversity and fairness are prioritized in all BI processes. Regular audits of algorithms can also help identify potential biases or issues that need to be addressed.

**Building a Culture of Responsibility**

Managing data privacy and ethical concerns isn't just a technical challenge, it's also a cultural one. Companies need to foster a culture where data privacy and ethics are taken seriously at every level of the organization. This starts with leadership setting the tone and ensuring that ethical considerations are integrated into the company's core values.

Training employees on data privacy laws and ethical data use is essential. When employees understand the importance of protecting customer data and making ethical decisions, they're more likely to approach their work with a sense of responsibility. This also helps prevent issues from arising due to negligence or lack of knowledge.

Additionally, companies should be transparent not only with their customers but also internally. Creating clear communication channels between departments about data usage and encouraging a collaborative approach to addressing privacy and ethical concerns can help create a more responsible data-driven culture.

Ultimately, managing data privacy and ethical concerns is an ongoing process. As BI technology continues to evolve, businesses must remain vigilant in protecting personal information, complying with regulations, and ensuring that their use of data reflects their values. By doing so, companies can build trust with their customers and stakeholders while maintaining the benefits of a data-driven approach.

---

Chapter 6

# Leveraging BI for Future Growth

## Predictive Analytics: Anticipating the Future

In business, staying one step ahead of competitors and customer needs is a game-changer. This is where predictive analytics becomes a powerful tool, enabling companies to anticipate future trends, behaviors, and challenges based on historical data. Rather than merely reacting to past events, businesses can use predictive analytics to make informed decisions that shape the future.

**How Predictive Analytics Works**

At its core, predictive analytics uses statistical techniques, machine learning algorithms, and historical data to forecast future outcomes. By identifying patterns and trends within large datasets, predictive analytics helps businesses understand what might happen next.

Imagine you run a retail business and want to prepare for the upcoming holiday season. Instead of simply stocking up based on last year's performance, you can use predictive analytics to analyze customer purchasing habits, current market trends, and external factors like economic conditions. This allows you to make data-driven predictions about which products will be in high demand and how much inventory to order, reducing the risk of overstocking or running out of key items.

**Anticipating Customer Behavior**

One of the most common uses of predictive analytics is in anticipating customer behavior. By analyzing past purchases, browsing patterns, and even social media interactions, businesses can predict what customers are likely to buy next, when they'll make their purchase, and how much they're willing to spend. This allows businesses to personalize marketing efforts and offer promotions that are more relevant to individual customers.

For example, streaming services like Netflix and Spotify use predictive analytics to recommend content based on your previous interactions. The system doesn't just look at what you've already watched or listened to—it analyzes the preferences of similar users to predict what you're likely to enjoy next. The result is a highly personalized experience that keeps customers engaged.

## Managing Risk and Reducing Uncertainty

Predictive analytics is also an invaluable tool for managing risk. In industries like finance and insurance, predicting future risks is essential to staying profitable. By analyzing historical data and identifying key risk factors, companies can anticipate potential challenges and take proactive measures to minimize them.

A bank, for instance, can use predictive analytics to assess the likelihood that a loan applicant will default based on their financial history and other relevant data. This allows the bank to make more informed lending decisions, reducing the risk of losses.

Similarly, businesses can use predictive analytics to forecast potential disruptions in their supply chains. By analyzing data from suppliers, transportation providers, and market conditions, companies can anticipate delays or shortages and take steps to mitigate the impact.

## Improving Operational Efficiency

Predictive analytics isn't just about understanding customers or managing risk—it can also be used to improve internal operations. Businesses can use predictive models to optimize everything from inventory management to staffing levels.

For instance, a restaurant might use predictive analytics to forecast customer traffic based on factors like the day of the week, weather, and local events. With this information, the restaurant can adjust staffing levels accordingly, ensuring they have enough employees to handle busy nights without overstaffing on slow ones.

In manufacturing, predictive analytics can be used to predict when machinery is likely to fail based on historical performance data. This allows companies to perform maintenance before a breakdown occurs, reducing downtime and improving overall efficiency.

## The Future of Predictive Analytics

As technology continues to evolve, predictive analytics is becoming even more powerful. With the rise of big data, artificial intelligence, and machine learning, businesses have access to larger datasets and more sophisticated algorithms, enabling even more accurate predictions.

In the near future, predictive analytics could become an integral part of every business decision, from product development to customer service strategies. Companies that embrace this technology will be better positioned to adapt to changes in the market, meet customer needs, and stay ahead of the competition.

Predictive analytics gives businesses the ability to anticipate the future, providing a competitive advantage in an increasingly fast-paced world. When used effectively, it transforms data into foresight, enabling organizations to make proactive decisions and seize new opportunities before others even see them coming.

## BI in Emerging Markets

Business Intelligence is proving to be a game-changer for companies operating in emerging markets. These regions, which often face unique challenges such as volatile economies, limited infrastructure, and rapidly shifting consumer preferences, are increasingly turning to BI to navigate these complexities. With the right data-driven strategies, businesses in emerging markets can make more informed decisions, gain a competitive edge, and drive sustainable growth.

**Unlocking Market Potential with Data**

Emerging markets, from Southeast Asia to Africa and Latin America, represent huge opportunities for businesses due to their growing populations and rising middle class. However, these regions also come with uncertainties and risks that can be difficult to manage without accurate, up-to-date information. This is where BI comes into play. By gathering data on local consumer behaviors, economic trends, and regulatory changes, companies can better understand the unique dynamics of these markets and adjust their strategies accordingly.

For instance, a company entering the African market might use BI to analyze mobile payment trends, as mobile banking has become a dominant force in many parts of the continent. By tracking these trends, businesses can tailor their offerings to meet local payment preferences and build stronger connections with customers.

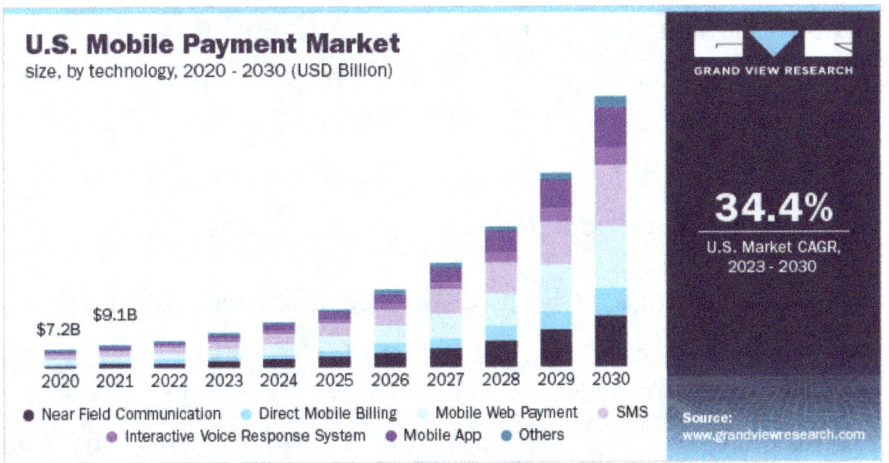

*Mobile Payment Trends in the U.S. Source: grandviewresearch.com*

## Navigating Economic Volatility

One of the key challenges in emerging markets is economic volatility. Fluctuations in currency, inflation rates, and local regulations can make it difficult for businesses to plan long-term strategies. BI helps companies navigate this uncertainty by providing real-time insights into economic conditions, enabling more agile decision-making.

For example, a company operating in Latin America might use BI to track currency fluctuations and adjust pricing strategies to protect profit margins. With a clearer understanding of the economic landscape, businesses can mitigate risks and remain competitive, even in unpredictable environments.

## Customizing Products and Services for Local Needs

Another advantage of BI in emerging markets is its ability to help companies tailor their products and services to local needs. Consumer preferences in emerging markets can vary significantly from those in developed countries, and a one-size-fits-all approach rarely works. BI tools allow businesses to gather and analyze data on local preferences, enabling them to customize their offerings more effectively.

For instance, a global retailer entering India might use BI to understand regional preferences for certain types of products or payment methods. With this data, the company can stock inventory that aligns with local demand and adjust its marketing campaigns to resonate with Indian consumers. This data-driven approach ensures that the business meets local expectations and strengthens its foothold in the market.

## Overcoming Infrastructure and Supply Chain Challenges

Infrastructure limitations are another common hurdle in emerging markets. Poor transportation networks, unreliable utilities, and other logistical challenges can disrupt supply chains and lead to inefficiencies. BI helps companies overcome these challenges by optimizing supply chain operations and identifying bottlenecks in the system.

For example, a company distributing goods across Southeast Asia could use BI to monitor real-time data on transportation routes, warehouse inventories, and delivery times. This information enables the business to streamline operations, reduce costs, and improve delivery times, even in regions with challenging infrastructure.

**Creating a Competitive Advantage**

In many emerging markets, businesses face stiff competition from both local and international players. BI provides a crucial competitive advantage by enabling companies to act quickly on market insights and outmaneuver competitors. Businesses that invest in BI can identify new opportunities faster, respond to changes in consumer behavior more effectively, and optimize their operations to outperform competitors who rely on traditional decision-making approaches.

For instance, a company in Brazil might use BI to monitor the actions of competitors, track shifts in consumer sentiment, and quickly pivot its marketing strategy to capture market share.

This ability to adapt quickly gives BI-driven businesses a significant edge in dynamic, fast-growing markets.

In emerging markets, BI is more than just a tool for improving efficiency; it is a strategic asset that enables businesses to navigate uncertainty, customize offerings, and gain a competitive edge. Companies that embrace BI in these regions are better positioned to capitalize on the immense opportunities they present.

## AI and Machine Learning in BI

Artificial Intelligence (AI) and Machine Learning (ML) are revolutionizing how businesses leverage data in BI. These technologies are no longer futuristic concepts; they're now integral components of modern BI systems, offering deeper insights and automation that enhance decision-making capabilities. AI and ML allow businesses to go beyond analyzing past performance and enable predictive and prescriptive insights that drive more effective strategies.

**How AI Enhances BI**

AI fundamentally changes the way data is processed in BI by automating tasks that traditionally required manual effort. In BI, AI-driven tools can process large volumes of data, find patterns, and present meaningful insights much faster than human analysis. Instead of spending hours sifting through data, businesses can rely on AI to uncover insights within minutes.

For example, a retail business might want to analyze customer sentiment from thousands of social media posts. Manually reviewing that data would take a huge amount of time, but an AI-powered BI tool can analyze the sentiment behind those posts—positive, neutral, or negative—almost instantly, allowing the company to quickly understand customer perceptions and adjust its strategies.

AI also excels at eliminating data silos by connecting disparate data sources, making it easier for companies to have a unified view of their operations. With this kind of data integration, decision-makers have all the necessary information in one place, empowering them to act on insights swiftly.

*Example of AI Integration in a BI Dashboard for Sentiment Analysis. Source: slideteam.net*

## Machine Learning and Predictive Capabilities

ML, a subset of AI, is particularly valuable in BI because it improves over time as it processes more data. This capability allows businesses to use historical data not just to understand the past but to predict future trends. ML algorithms can recognize complex patterns that humans might overlook, enabling businesses to forecast outcomes with greater accuracy.

For instance, an e-commerce company can use ML to predict customer churn. By analyzing past customer behavior, such as frequency of purchases, customer support interactions, and browsing patterns, ML models can predict which customers are at risk of leaving. With this knowledge, the business can take proactive steps to re-engage those customers before they churn.

In addition to predicting behavior, ML can be used to optimize operations. A manufacturing company might use ML algorithms to predict when machinery is likely to fail, allowing the company to perform maintenance at the right time. This approach reduces downtime and ensures the production line operates smoothly.

## Personalization and Customer Experience

One of the most impactful applications of AI and ML in BI is the ability to personalize customer experiences. Companies like Amazon and Netflix have set the standard for using data to recommend products or content based on individual preferences. This level of personalization is now within reach for businesses of all sizes, thanks to AI and ML.

For example, an online retailer can use AI to analyze a customer's browsing history, purchase patterns, and even weather conditions in their location. Based on this data, the retailer can recommend products that are likely to appeal to the customer at that specific moment. Personalization not only enhances the customer experience but also drives higher engagement and sales.

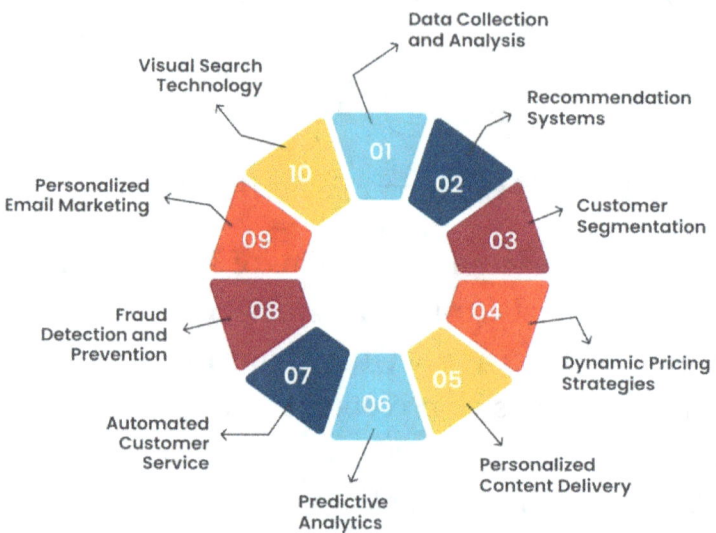

Components of Personalized Powered by AI and ML in E-commerce. Source: jellyfishtechnologies.com

**Automating BI Processes**

AI and ML also play a key role in automating repetitive BI tasks, freeing up time for analysts and decision-makers to focus on more strategic activities. BI platforms with AI capabilities can automate tasks like data cleansing, report generation, and anomaly detection. For example, if there is an unexpected spike in website traffic, an AI-powered system can automatically alert the team, flag the issue, and provide potential reasons for the anomaly based on historical data.

This automation reduces the need for manual intervention, speeds up decision-making, and ensures that businesses can respond quickly to changing conditions. In industries where time-sensitive decisions are critical, such as finance or retail, this capability is especially valuable.

**The Future of AI and ML in BI**

As AI and ML technologies continue to evolve, their role in BI will only grow. Future advancements will likely include even more sophisticated predictive models, deeper integration with real-time data sources, and enhanced automation features that reduce human input while delivering more precise insights.

AI and ML will also make BI more accessible to businesses that don't have large teams of data scientists. With user-friendly AI-driven BI platforms, even small businesses can harness the power of these technologies without needing specialized technical expertise.

In the world of BI, AI and ML aren't just buzzwords, they're tools that are transforming how businesses operate, offering deeper insights, faster decisions, and more personalized customer experiences. The integration of these technologies into BI platforms represents a major leap forward in the way businesses use data to drive success.

Chapter 7

# Actionable Strategies for Implementing BI

## Creating a BI-Driven Culture

Adopting BI tools is only the first step toward making data-driven decisions, but for BI to truly transform an organization, it must become part of the company's culture. Creating a BI-driven culture means fostering an environment where data is not only accessible but also embraced at every level of the business. Leaders must encourage employees to rely on data to inform their decisions and ensure that BI tools are fully integrated into daily operations. This section explores how companies can successfully embed BI into their culture, making it a central component of the decision-making process.

**Leadership Commitment to Data-Driven Decision-Making**

A BI-driven culture starts at the top. Leadership plays a key role in setting the tone for how data is valued and used across the organization. When executives and managers consistently base their decisions on data, it sends a strong message to employees that BI is essential to the company's success. Leaders should not only use BI tools themselves but also openly discuss the insights gained from data during meetings and strategy sessions. This demonstrates a commitment to data-driven decision-making and encourages others to follow suit.

In addition to leading by example, executives should invest in the necessary infrastructure and resources to support a data-driven culture. This includes providing access to BI tools, offering training programs, and ensuring that employees have the support they need to use these tools effectively. The more leadership emphasizes the importance of BI, the more likely it is that the entire organization will adopt and embrace it.

**Making Data Accessible Across the Organization**

For BI to become part of the company's culture, data must be easily accessible to employees at all levels. If data is only available to a select few, it's difficult to foster widespread adoption. Companies need to break down barriers to data access, ensuring that employees in different departments can easily retrieve and analyze the information they need.

This might involve integrating various data sources into a unified BI platform that provides employees with a single point of access. When employees can quickly pull up relevant data, they are more likely to use it in their decision-making processes.

Additionally, simplifying BI tools and making them user-friendly is crucial. Complex systems that require specialized skills can discourage employees from engaging with data. Intuitive dashboards and visualizations can help make data more accessible, empowering more employees to use it in their daily work.

**Encouraging a Mindset Shift**

Shifting to a BI-driven culture also requires a change in mindset. In many organizations, employees are used to relying on gut instincts or experience when making decisions. Encouraging them to shift toward data-driven thinking requires not only training but also clear communication about the value of data. Employees need to understand that BI is not replacing their expertise, but enhancing it. Data provides valuable insights that complement their knowledge, helping them make better, more informed decisions.

One way to encourage this mindset shift is through success stories. Highlight examples where data-driven decisions led to positive outcomes within the company, such as improved sales, better customer experiences, or operational efficiencies. These stories can motivate employees to embrace data in their own roles and see the practical benefits of a BI-driven approach.

## Continuous Training and Development

A BI-driven culture is not built overnight, and continuous learning is essential to its success. Employees must feel confident using BI tools, which means investing in ongoing training and development. Regular workshops, tutorials, and hands-on sessions can help employees stay up-to-date with the latest features of BI platforms and ensure they are making the most of the data at their disposal.

Training should not only focus on how to use BI tools but also on how to interpret data and turn it into actionable insights. Employees need to be able to analyze the information effectively and understand how it applies to their specific roles. By providing the necessary resources and fostering an environment of learning, companies can ensure that employees at all levels are equipped to use BI in meaningful ways.

## Celebrating Data-Driven Successes

Celebrating the success of data-driven decisions can reinforce the importance of BI within the company culture. Recognizing teams or individuals who have effectively used data to achieve great results can serve as inspiration for others. This could be done through internal newsletters, company meetings, or awards that highlight the value of data in driving business success.

When employees see their efforts rewarded and celebrated, they are more likely to continue using data in their decision-making processes. This positive reinforcement helps cement BI as a cornerstone of the company's culture and encourages others to follow suit.

By embedding BI into the very fabric of the organization, businesses can create a culture where data is valued, used, and embraced at every level. From leadership commitment to continuous employee training, building a BI-driven culture requires effort, but the rewards—a more agile, informed, and competitive organization—are well worth it.

## Customizing BI Solutions for Your Business

No two businesses are exactly alike, so why should their BI solutions be the same? Customizing BI for your business ensures that the insights you gather are not just relevant but actionable, directly addressing your unique challenges, goals, and industry-specific requirements. A one-size-fits-all approach might get you started, but a tailored BI solution will help your business truly thrive.

## Understanding Your Business Needs

The first step in customizing a BI solution is understanding the specific needs of your business. Are you looking to improve operational efficiency, enhance customer engagement, or boost sales? Different industries and businesses have different priorities, so your BI system must be designed to align with your goals.

For example, a retail business might need real-time insights into inventory levels and customer purchasing trends, while a manufacturing company might focus on optimizing supply chain efficiency and minimizing downtime in production. Taking the time to identify your key business drivers will ensure that the data you collect and analyze serves your overall objectives.

## Choosing the Right BI Tools

Not all BI tools are created equal, and selecting the right platform is essential for a customized solution. Many BI platforms offer a wide range of features, but some may be more suited to your specific business environment than others. For instance, if your company heavily relies on real-time data to make decisions, you'll want a BI platform that excels in providing real-time dashboards and alerts. If your team requires advanced data visualization tools to communicate complex insights to stakeholders, that should be a primary consideration.

Another factor to consider is the level of technical expertise within your team. Some BI tools are designed for users with minimal technical knowledge, offering simple drag-and-drop functionality, while others provide advanced customization options for more tech-savvy teams. Choose a tool that matches your team's skill level and the complexity of the data you're working with.

**Integrating BI with Your Existing Systems**

For BI to be truly effective, it needs to integrate seamlessly with the systems you already have in place. Whether you're using an ERP system, CRM software, or a cloud-based database, your BI tool should be able to pull data from these sources without creating bottlenecks or compatibility issues. Many BI platforms offer integrations with popular business software, but you may need to customize these integrations to ensure they work for your specific setup.

For example, if you're running a retail business, your BI system should integrate with your point-of-sale system, your inventory management software, and any customer loyalty programs you have in place. By pulling data from all these sources, you'll be able to gain a more holistic view of your business operations and make more informed decisions.

## Designing Custom Dashboards and Reports

Once you've set up your BI system, it's time to design the dashboards and reports that will deliver the insights you need. Custom dashboards allow you to focus on the metrics that matter most to your business. A sales manager might want to see daily sales trends and customer acquisition rates, while an operations manager may focus on supply chain performance and production efficiency.

Dashboards can be tailored to suit different roles within the company, ensuring that each department has access to the insights that are most relevant to them. Custom reports, meanwhile, allow you to delve deeper into specific areas of the business. These reports can be scheduled to run automatically, providing regular updates on key performance indicators or generating detailed analysis on demand.

## Adapting BI as Your Business Grows

Your BI solution shouldn't remain static. As your business evolves, your BI tools and strategies need to adapt to new challenges and opportunities. For example, if your company expands into new markets, your BI system should be able to track performance in different regions and adjust metrics to reflect local trends and customer behavior.

Similarly, as your business collects more data, you may need to implement more advanced BI features, such as machine learning or predictive analytics, to keep up with the growing complexity. Customization isn't a one-time effort—it's an ongoing process that ensures your BI solution remains aligned with your business needs over time.

Customizing a BI solution for your business isn't just about picking the right tools, it's about ensuring those tools work for your unique situation. With the right approach, your BI system can evolve alongside your company, delivering valuable insights that drive growth, efficiency, and success.

## Scaling BI Solutions as Your Business Grows

As businesses grow, their BI needs evolve. What starts as a simple tool to analyze sales data can quickly turn into a complex system that tracks customer behavior, forecasts demand, and optimizes supply chains. Scaling BI solutions is crucial for businesses that want to maintain their competitive edge while ensuring their operations run smoothly.

## Adapting to Increased Data Volume

When businesses expand, the amount of data they collect grows exponentially. More customers, transactions, and touchpoints result in vast amounts of information flowing into the system. Scaling BI to accommodate this growth involves ensuring the infrastructure can handle larger data sets without slowing down or compromising accuracy.

At this stage, businesses often move from smaller, more basic BI platforms to more robust solutions that can process and analyze large datasets in real time. Cloud-based BI solutions are particularly useful for growing businesses, as they allow for flexibility and scalability without requiring significant upfront investment in hardware. These platforms can be expanded as needed, with additional processing power or storage allocated as the business grows.

## Maintaining Data Quality Across Systems

As businesses scale, they often adopt new systems and platforms, leading to fragmented data. A common challenge during growth is maintaining data quality and consistency across multiple sources. For instance, a company may have separate systems for sales, marketing, and customer service, each collecting different data points. Without proper integration, this can lead to discrepancies and errors in BI reports.

To address this, businesses need to invest in data integration solutions that bring information from various sources into a unified BI platform. This ensures that data remains consistent, accurate, and up-to-date, regardless of which department or system it originates from. A well-integrated system allows decision-makers to trust the insights they're getting and make informed choices based on comprehensive, real-time data.

**Expanding BI Usage Across Departments**

When businesses are small, BI might be confined to a few key departments, such as finance or marketing. However, as the organization grows, the need for data-driven insights expands across all areas—HR, logistics, product development, and beyond. Scaling BI means making data accessible to every department, empowering more teams to leverage insights for better decision-making.

For example, the HR department could use BI to track employee performance and optimize hiring strategies, while the logistics team could analyze transportation routes to reduce delivery times and costs. To support this, companies should invest in user-friendly BI tools that require minimal technical expertise, allowing employees in various roles to easily access and analyze data.

**Ensuring Security and Compliance**

As businesses scale their BI solutions, they must also ensure that data privacy and security protocols scale with them. Larger datasets and more users accessing the system mean an increased risk of security breaches. Companies need to implement robust security measures, including encryption, user access controls, and regular audits, to protect sensitive data.

Additionally, as companies expand into new markets, they may face varying data privacy regulations. Compliance with local laws, such as the GDPR in Europe or the CCPA in California, becomes more complex as businesses grow. Scalable BI solutions should have built-in compliance features to ensure that the company adheres to all relevant regulations, regardless of where the data is being collected or processed.

**Fostering a Data-Driven Culture as You Scale**

As BI becomes more central to the business, it's important to foster a culture that embraces data at every level. This means continuing to invest in training and development, so employees feel confident using BI tools. It also means encouraging data-driven decision-making, where teams across the organization are empowered to leverage insights to improve processes, innovate, and drive growth.

Creating a scalable BI infrastructure isn't just about technology, it's about building a company-wide commitment to using data as a strategic asset. As your business grows, scaling BI solutions ensures that you stay agile, informed, and prepared for the challenges and opportunities ahead.

# Conclusion

Throughout this book, we have explored how BI can be a transformative force for businesses of all sizes, across various industries and markets. From understanding the foundations of BI and implementing data-driven strategies across business functions to overcoming the challenges of data silos and privacy concerns, each section has provided actionable insights on how to leverage data for better decision-making.

The core message of this book is simple: in today's world, data is one of the most valuable assets a business can have. But the power of data only comes to life when it is harnessed through BI systems that can turn raw information into actionable insights. As businesses grow, expand into new markets, and face increasing competition, those that make data-driven decisions will be the ones to thrive.

The significance of embracing BI is not just about improving operations or predicting trends—it's about fundamentally changing how businesses think and operate. BI allows leaders to make smarter, faster, and more informed decisions, giving them the agility and foresight needed to navigate an ever-changing business landscape. By creating a BI-driven culture, integrating data across departments, and scaling BI solutions as your business grows, you are setting the foundation for long-term success.

As you finish this book, I encourage you to take the next step: apply the insights and strategies you've learned here. Whether it's improving your supply chain efficiency, personalizing customer experiences, or empowering your teams with data-driven tools, you now have the knowledge to transform your business with BI. The future of business is data-driven—so embrace it, leverage it, and use it to create a more informed, agile, and competitive organization. The decisions you make today will shape your business tomorrow.

Dear Reader,

I hope you found the book insightful and valuable.

Your feedback is invaluable to me. If you enjoyed reading this book, I would appreciate it if you could take a moment to leave a review on the reading apps and platforms.

Thank you for your support, and I wish you all the best.

Kind regards,
Ghazwan

# About the Author

Ghazwan is a passionate entrepreneur and business strategist dedicated to helping individuals and organizations achieve their full potential with a deep understanding of modern businesses' challenges and opportunities.

With a Master's degree in Computer and Systems Sciences from Stockholm University, specializing in eService design, requirement engineering, and business process management, he is equipped to innovate cutting-edge solutions.

He believes in the power of collaboration and lifelong learning, and his mission is to empower people to reach their goals and positively impact the world.

www.ingramcontent.com/pod-product-compliance
Lightning Source LLC
Chambersburg PA
CBHW071037240526
45469CB00006BD/2235